this coupon is g

GW01374746

_____

_____

_____

NO EXPIRY. NON TRANSFERABLE. CAN BE REDEEMED ONCE ONLY.

with love

from

———————————————————

to

———————————————————

this coupon is good for

_____

_____

_____

NO EXPIRY. NON TRANSFERABLE. CAN BE REDEEMED ONCE ONLY.

with love

from

---

to

this coupon is good for

_____

_____

_____

NO EXPIRY. NON TRANSFERABLE. CAN BE REDEEMED ONCE ONLY.

with love

from

to

this coupon is good for

_____

_____

_____

NO EXPIRY. NON TRANSFERABLE. CAN BE REDEEMED ONCE ONLY.

with love

from

---

to

this coupon is good for

_____

_____

_____

NO EXPIRY. NON TRANSFERABLE. CAN BE REDEEMED ONCE ONLY.

with love

from

_____

to

_____

this coupon is good for

_____

_____

_____

NO EXPIRY. NON TRANSFERABLE. CAN BE REDEEMED ONCE ONLY.

with love

from

_____

to

_____

this coupon is good for

_____

_____

_____

NO EXPIRY. NON TRANSFERABLE. CAN BE REDEEMED ONCE ONLY.

with love

from

___

to

___

this coupon is good for

NO EXPIRY. NON TRANSFERABLE. CAN BE REDEEMED ONCE ONLY.

with love

from

_____

to

_____

this coupon is good for

_____

_____

_____

NO EXPIRY. NON TRANSFERABLE. CAN BE REDEEMED ONCE ONLY.

with love

from

to

this coupon is good for

_____

_____

_____

NO EXPIRY. NON TRANSFERABLE. CAN BE REDEEMED ONCE ONLY.

with love

from

to

this coupon is good for

_____

_____

_____

NO EXPIRY. NON TRANSFERABLE. CAN BE REDEEMED ONCE ONLY.

with love

from

to

this coupon is good for

_____

_____

_____

NO EXPIRY. NON TRANSFERABLE. CAN BE REDEEMED ONCE ONLY.

with love

from

to

this coupon is good for

_____

_____

_____

NO EXPIRY. NON TRANSFERABLE. CAN BE REDEEMED ONCE ONLY.

with love

from

to

this coupon is good for

NO EXPIRY. NON TRANSFERABLE. CAN BE REDEEMED ONCE ONLY.

with love

from

to

this coupon is good for

_____

_____

_____

NO EXPIRY. NON TRANSFERABLE. CAN BE REDEEMED ONCE ONLY.

with love

from

to

this coupon is good for

NO EXPIRY. NON TRANSFERABLE. CAN BE REDEEMED ONCE ONLY.

with love

from

to

this coupon is good for

_____

_____

_____

NO EXPIRY. NON TRANSFERABLE. CAN BE REDEEMED ONCE ONLY.

with love

from

to

this coupon is good for

_____

_____

_____

NO EXPIRY. NON TRANSFERABLE. CAN BE REDEEMED ONCE ONLY.

with love

from

to

this coupon is good for

_____

_____

_____

NO EXPIRY. NON TRANSFERABLE. CAN BE REDEEMED ONCE ONLY.

with love

from

to

this coupon is good for

_____

_____

_____

NO EXPIRY. NON TRANSFERABLE. CAN BE REDEEMED ONCE ONLY.

with love

from

_____

to

_____

this coupon is good for

_____

_____

_____

NO EXPIRY. NON TRANSFERABLE. CAN BE REDEEMED ONCE ONLY.

with love

from

to

this coupon is good for

_____

_____

_____

NO EXPIRY. NON TRANSFERABLE. CAN BE REDEEMED ONCE ONLY.

with love

from

to

this coupon is good for

NO EXPIRY. NON TRANSFERABLE. CAN BE REDEEMED ONCE ONLY.

with love

from

to

this coupon is good for

_____

_____

_____

NO EXPIRY. NON TRANSFERABLE. CAN BE REDEEMED ONCE ONLY.

with love

from

---

to

this coupon is good for

_____

_____

_____

NO EXPIRY. NON TRANSFERABLE. CAN BE REDEEMED ONCE ONLY.

with love

from

to

this coupon is good for

_____

_____

_____

NO EXPIRY. NON TRANSFERABLE. CAN BE REDEEMED ONCE ONLY.

with love

from

---

to

this coupon is good for

_____

_____

_____

NO EXPIRY. NON TRANSFERABLE. CAN BE REDEEMED ONCE ONLY.

with love

⇢ *from* ⇠

_____

⇢ *to* ⇠

_____

this coupon is good for

_____

_____

_____

NO EXPIRY. NON TRANSFERABLE. CAN BE REDEEMED ONCE ONLY.

with love

from

to

this coupon is good for

_____

_____

_____

NO EXPIRY. NON TRANSFERABLE. CAN BE REDEEMED ONCE ONLY.

with love

from

_____

to

_____

this coupon is good for

_____

_____

_____

NO EXPIRY. NON TRANSFERABLE. CAN BE REDEEMED ONCE ONLY.

with love

from

_____

to

_____

Printed in Great Britain
by Amazon